PAPER AND TAPE CRAFTS

PAPER AND TAPE CRAFTS

28 Inventive Activities for Kids Ages 8-12

JENNIFER PERKINS

ROCKRIDGE
PRESS

First Rockridge Press trade paperback edition 2023

Rockridge Press and the Rockridge Press logo are trademarks or registered trademarks of Callisto Media Inc. and/or its affiliates in the United States and other countries and may not be used without written permission.

For general information on our other products and services, please contact our Customer Care Department within the United States at (866) 744-2665, or outside the United States at (510) 253-0500.

Paperback ISBN: 979-8-88608-055-1 | eBook ISBN: 979-8-88650-194-0

Manufactured in the United States of America

Interior and Cover Designer: Angela Navarra
Art Producer: Sue Bischofberger
Editor: Maxine Marshall
Production Editor: Jael Fogle
Production Manager: Lanore Coloprisco

Illustrations © Ruslana Lubenets/Creative Market: (stripes); © Bibadash/Shutterstock (design elements); © Peter Hermes Furian/Shutterstock: 1 (map)

10 9 8 7 6 5 4 3 2 1 0

TATER AND TOT
This book,
like most everything I do,
is for you guys.

CONTENTS

HELLO, CRAFTER!

With some tape, scissors, and paper, you can make a snake or tell your best friend's fortune. Grab a few paper lunch bags and a hole punch. Now you're making miniature cities. Is it possible to make 28 cool projects with just a few supplies you can find around the house? Keep reading, and I'll show you how!

My name is Jennifer Perkins, and I like to craft . . . a lot. I discovered my love for glue as a kid and have never looked back. As an adult, I have used that love to write books, edit a kids' craft magazine, host television shows, and create content for places like HGTV and Michaels.

Best of all, I have a son who likes to craft. My son inspired many of the projects in this book, like the magazine mountain for toy cars to drive around and the silly-face flip-book. These crafts are fun and quick. In minutes, you will be able to whip up a cardboard airplane or a paper-ball version of Saturn.

Each of the 28 projects here includes step-by-step instructions and a list of supplies you'll need, plus pictures to help you see exactly how to make it. There are also notes at the end of each project. Craft Re-Creation notes offer ideas for using different materials or making the project a different way. Craft Up notes challenge you to take the craft further or to expand on what you've already done.

I promise (and I know from experience) that this is the perfect book to keep you busy and entertained. These projects are just as fun to play with as they are to make.

Now, let's get crafty!

NOTES ON SAFETY

Safety first! Most of the craft supplies in this book are easy to use and nontoxic. That doesn't mean you shouldn't be careful. Take care when cutting with scissors and when walking around with them. The metal part on tape dispensers is another sharp edge that can cut. Take your time, use common sense, and ask an adult for help when you need it.

Reading the labels when crafting is always a good idea. Take a look at the labels on paint, markers, and glue if you decide to use these supplies to decorate any of your projects. The AP Seal on craft supplies means that the item is certified nontoxic by the Art and Creative Materials Institute.

SUPPLIES: SUPERCOOL PAPERS AND TAPES

Most of the projects in this book can be made with plain white printer paper and clear adhesive tape, but it is fun to add color. Chances are you have a few items around the house that you can use to take your crafts to the next level. You might like to have these materials on hand, too.

PAPER SUPPLIES

Cardboard boxes, like empty cereal boxes

Cardboard paper towel tubes or cardboard toilet paper tubes

Cardstock, in several colors

Construction paper, in several colors

Crepe paper streamers

Glitter craft paper

Magazines

Newspaper

Paper lunch bags

Paper plates

Paper straws

Patterned scrapbooking paper

Poster board

Printed napkins

Printer paper

Tissue paper, in several colors

Wax paper

TAPE SUPPLIES

Clear adhesive tape (like Scotch Brand tape)

Clear packing tape

Double-sided tape

Duct tape

Washi tape, in a variety of colors and patterns

SUPPLIES: HANDY TOOLS AND EXTRAS

A few crafts in the book call for simple tools, like a hole punch or a craft needle (a big sewing needle). All the tools needed in the book are listed here. In addition, while paper and tape take center stage in every craft, some projects require a bit of yarn or a paper clip. Use this list to plan for extra materials that are used in some of the crafts or that are mentioned in the Crafty Recreation and Craft Up tips.

TOOLS

Circular objects for tracing, such as cups and jars

Craft needle

Hole punch

Paintbrush

Pencil or pen

Ruler

Scissors

OTHER MATERIALS

Ball head straight pins

Decoupage medium (like Mod Podge)

Glue stick

Ice pop sticks

LED string lights

LED tea light

Markers, crayons, and/or paints

Paper clips

Rubber bands

White school glue

World map poster or printout

Yarn

WORLDLY WASHI MAP PINS

WHAT YOU'LL NEED

- Washi tape
- Ruler
- Ball head straight pins
- Scissors
- World map poster or printout

Do you dream of traveling the world? Maybe you have visited a few fun destinations already. Poke these pins into a map as a visual reminder of your adventures in the big and wonderful world. Consider using one color of pin to mark places you've been and another to mark places you'd love to go. continued >>

INSTRUCTIONS

1. Tear off a strip of washi tape about 5 inches long.

2. Lay the washi tape, sticky side facing up, on a flat surface.

3. Place a pin in the center of the strip of tape with the ball head of the pin right above the strip of tape.

4. Fold the washi tape together, making sure you get a good seal around the pin. If the sides do not meet up evenly on your first fold, unstick the tape and try again.

5. Using scissors, trim your washi tape flag to a size you prefer.

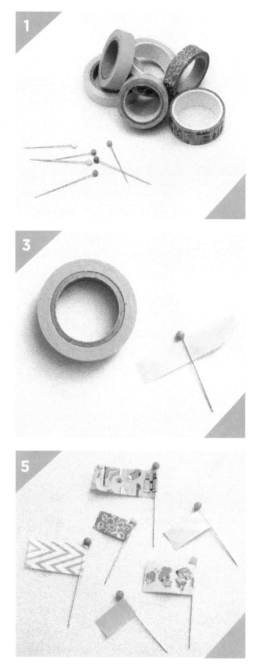

6. Cut a small triangle shape out of the end of the washi tape to make your pin look like a flag.

7. Stick the pins into your map to mark places you've been or would like to visit. This will work best if your map is attached to a corkboard or something else pins will go into easily. Be sure to ask permission before poking pins into any surface.

CRAFTY RE-CREATION: If you don't have washi tape, paper works great, too. Cut small strips of paper to fold over your pin. Use double-sided tape or a bit of glue to attach the two sides of the paper strip together. Trim and cut out your triangle just as you would with washi tape.

CRAFT UP: Extra ambitious aspiring travelers can attach mini flags to their map pins. Print out small pictures of the flags of different countries. Cut out the pictures and attach them to your pins with tape. Or try drawing the flags onto small pieces of paper with markers or colored pencils.

PAPER BAG CITY

WHAT YOU'LL NEED

- Scissors
- 3 to 5 paper lunch bags
- Washi tape in several colors
- 3 to 5 sheets cardstock
- Ruler
- Newspaper
- Clear adhesive tape

You might have thought brown paper bags were just for school lunches. That was before you took your cars for a spin around Paper Bag City! You'll explore the wonders of colorful washi tape as you create artsy architecture.

INSTRUCTIONS

1. Use scissors to trim the tops of a few paper bags so that they are all different heights. You can also use different size bags if you have them.

2. Lay the bags flat. Use strips of washi tape to create squares and rectangles on them that will be windows and doors.

3. Use another color of washi tape to create door frames, windowpanes, and other accents. Set the bags aside.

4. Use the ruler and scissors to cut cardstock rectangles that are roughly 1 inch wider than the bags on every side. These are the roofs for the buildings; cut one roof for each bag.

5. Fold the cardstock rectangles in half. Set them aside.

continued >>

6. Stand the bags up, as if you were going to pack them. Place a small wad of newspaper inside each bag. This will help the bags stand.

7. Use clear adhesive tape to secure the cardstock roofs to the paper bag houses. Or you can place the roofs on top of the bags without taping them so you can fold your bags back up to store them after you're done playing.

CRAFTY RE-CREATION: Any type of bag with a flat bottom will work for this project. Black gift bags can become creepy haunted houses and colorful gift bags can be transformed into beautiful multicolored row houses.

CRAFT UP: Why stop at washi tape? Try using paint on your paper bags to create a city in a rainbow of colors. Use markers to draw brick facades and extra details on the houses. Think outside the city! By the way, paper bags make great gnome homes and little log cabins, too.

WASHI TAPE STICKERS

WHAT YOU'LL NEED

- Wax paper
- Washi tape
- Marker
- Scissors

Everybody loves stickers! With just a few supplies you can make your own. They look great on notebooks, are the perfect decoration on a letter, and are fun to trade with friends. continued >>

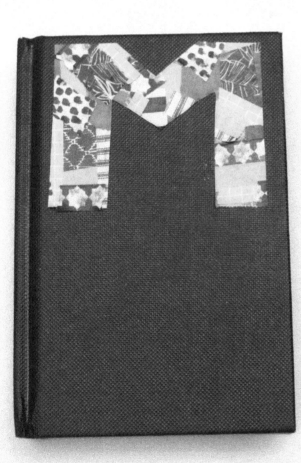

INSTRUCTIONS

1. Grab a small sheet of wax paper and set it on a flat surface.

2. Cover the wax paper with washi tape. Using small torn pieces, create a random pattern. Make sure to overlap the pieces of tape so you are creating one large sheet of washi.

3. When the wax paper is completely covered in washi tape, turn it over so the tape side is facing down and the wax paper side is facing up.

4. Using the marker, draw or trace shapes onto the wax paper. Basic shapes like stars and circles work best. If you want to make letter-shaped stickers, write the letters backwards so the letter will be facing the right way when you flip the sheet over.

5. Cut out the shapes.

6. When you are ready to use your stickers, gently remove the wax paper backing from the sticker and apply.

CRAFTY RE-CREATION: If this confetti pattern is not your style, try something different with your stickers. Stripes of washi tape are awfully striking, and there is nothing wrong with solid-colored stickers if you just want to use one roll of washi.

CRAFT UP: If you have paper punches, these wax paper sheets of washi tape have even more possibilities. Punch out shapes and use these stickers just about anywhere you might put a store-bought sticker. These are not waterproof stickers, so avoid attaching them to things like water bottles.

TEST YOUR MEMORY CARD GAME

WHAT YOU'LL NEED

- Ruler
- Pencil
- 1 sheet poster board
- Scissors
- Sheets or scraps of patterned scrapbooking paper, in at least 24 colors or patterns
- Double-sided tape

Chances are you have played a version of this matching memory game before. This do-it-yourself version is as fun to make as it is to play! Enjoy creating this lightweight and portable game to bring along on your next camping trip or over to a friend's house. You will need 24 different styles of patterned paper. Scraps work great.

INSTRUCTIONS

1. Using a ruler and pencil, draw 48 2½-inch squares on one side of the poster board.

2. Cut out the squares and set them aside.

3. Using a ruler, draw two 2½-inch squares on each piece of patterned paper. Be sure the two pieces you cut from the same paper match.

4. Cut out the patterned squares and set them aside.

5. Using double-sided tape, attach one square of patterned paper to each square of poster board.

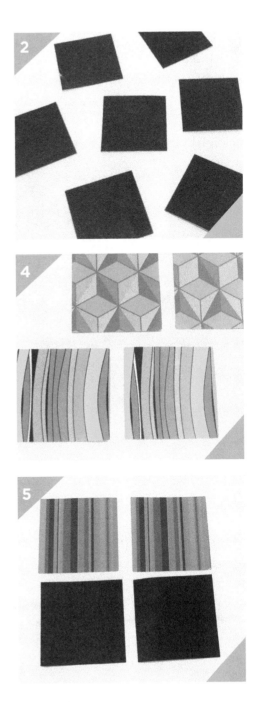

continued >>

6. To play the game, spread all the squares out on a flat sur-face with the poster board side up. Each player takes a turn flipping over two squares. If the patterns match, the player keeps those squares. If they do not match, the player turns the squares back over and the next player takes a turn. The goal is to collect the most matches.

CRAFTY RE-CREATION: Turn this game into a great hand-made gift with family photos. Print two copies each of 24 square photos. (Be sure to make them all the same size!) Cut out 48 poster-board squares that are the same size as the photos and attach the photos with double-sided tape. The rules of the game are the same.

CRAFT UP: Get creative with the patterned paper you use. Try notebook paper, aluminum foil, colorful paper napkins, and newspapers. When you start looking around the house, who knows what you'll find?

MAGAZINE MOUNTAINS

WHAT YOU'LL NEED

- Magazines
- Ruler
- Pencil
- Scissors
- Double-sided tape
- Binder clips (optional)

You may not be able to move mountains, but you can make them! This fun project is recycling at its best. Use old magazines to create a cool mountain terrain. They're perfect for building imaginary worlds or taking remote-control cars for a spin. Vary the size of your mountains by leaving some magazines intact and trimming off different amounts from others. Be sure to ask permission before cutting up the magazines. continued >>

INSTRUCTIONS

1. Start by opening a magazine to the center and using a ruler to measure 1 inch from the top of the page. Draw a line across the top, then cut off the strip you just measured, all the way across both pages. If your magazine is too thick you can do this a few pages at a time, using

your first cut as a guide. Cutting through the spine of the magazine will be the hardest part. Vary the size of your mountains by cutting off different size strips from different magazines. Before cutting, you can secure the magazine pages with binder clips for a cleaner look, if desired.

2. When you have trimmed a few magazines to different heights, begin making your mountains. Open a magazine to a page near the middle. Bend the top corner of the page over to the center spine. The folded part will form a triangle. Don't crease the outside edge; leave

it rounded, like a bubble. Tuck the edge of the sheet into the spine.

3. Repeat with the next page. The pages will stay in place more easily as you fold more pages. Continue until you have folded every page in the entire magazine.

4. When you reach the covers, finish your mountain by attaching the folded covers to each other with double-sided tape. One long strip between the two pages should work. Trim off any excess paper so you have a neat, cone-shaped mountain.

CRAFTY RE-CREATION: Would you prefer to make a forest? Go for it! This process doesn't only create mountains. Your cones can become pine trees, pyramids, or even yurts. Experiment with size to create a scene from your imagination.

CRAFT UP: Try painting your mountains. When you have everything assembled, brush on several light layers of brown paint. Allow for drying time between. Add white paint on top for a snow-capped look. Brrr!

MASKED MAKER

WHAT YOU'LL NEED

- 2 to 3 sheets cardstock, in several colors
- Pencil
- Scissors
- Double-sided tape
- Hole punch
- Yarn

If you've got paper and scissors, you can create a whole new you . . . or at least a masked version of yourself. Will you be a bird, a tiger, a creature you create? Let your imagination run wild.

INSTRUCTIONS

1. Draw and cut out the shape of a basic mask from a sheet of cardstock. A sideways number 8 is a good shape for a basic mask; just make sure the circles are large enough to cover more than your eyes. If you have a sleep mask, you can use that shape as a guide.

2. Place the mask over your eyes and ask a partner to use a pencil to gently mark where your eye holes need to be. Hold the mask away from your face and cut out the eye holes.

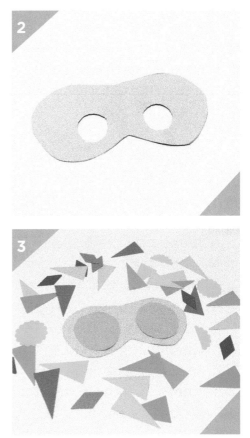

3. Cut shapes out of colorful cardstock paper. You will use these colored shapes to decorate your mask. Triangles, circles, and shapes of your own creation are great options. You might want to think about a theme or idea for your mask before you begin cutting. The photos here show a colorful bird theme.

continued >>

4. When you have several shapes cut out, use double-sided tape to attach the shapes to the mask. Don't cover the eye holes.

5. Use a hole punch to make holes on the two outside edges of the mask. You will use these holes to attach a strap.

6. Cut two pieces of yarn that are long enough to go all the way around your head. Fold one piece of yarn in half and pull the folded end through the hole. Tie a knot large enough that it will not slip back through the hole. Do the same with the other piece of yarn in the other hole. Leave enough yarn so that you can tie the mask behind your head.

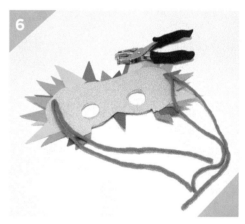

CRAFTY RE-CREATION: Try making a magazine mash-up mask. Follow steps 1 and 2 to cut out the basic mask shape. Then grab a stack of old magazines. Flip through them to find large photos of people. Cut out the hair from one photo, the eyes from another, and the mouth from a third. These can become the features on your mask. The wackier the mash-up, the wilder your mask will look.

CRAFT UP: You can make a mask with full face coverage. Follow the same process as for steps 1 and 2, but cut a larger base shape and cut holes for your nose and mouth before you start decorating.

CARDBOARD STACKERS

WHAT YOU'LL NEED

- 1 large cardboard box
- Scissors
- Pencil
- Washi tape
- Ruler

Have you ever built a tower or fort out of empty cardboard boxes? Making these interlocking blocks will take your building adventures to the next level. Big or small, round or square, decorated or not, the more shapes you make, the bigger and more elaborate your creations can be.

INSTRUCTIONS

1. Break down your cardboard box with scissors so you have several flat pieces to work with. Ask an adult for help if needed.

2. Draw several different shapes onto the flattened pieces of cardboard. Cardboard can be tricky to cut, so avoid intricate designs with small details. Shapes like ovals, stars, rectangles, and squares are great options.

3. Using scissors, cut out the shapes.

4. With washi tape, decorate the cardboard shapes to add stripes, polka dots, plaid patterns, or whatever you like.

5. Cut slits into the cardboard shapes so that the shapes can interlock. Cut slits that are about ½ inch long into two or three different spots on each piece of cardboard.

continued >>

6. Match up the slits on different pieces to connect them and build your free-form structure. The height of your tower will depend on how wide and strong your base is, as well as how many pieces of cardboard you use.

CRAFTY RE-CREATION: Washi tape is great for adding color and pizzazz. But don't worry if you don't have any around. Markers, pens, and paint work just as well to decorate your cardboard stackers. If you use paint or markers, be sure to let them dry before you start cutting and stacking.

CRAFT UP: Ever heard of decoupage? It's a fancy word for the process of attaching decorative paper to things. Using decoupage medium (an all-in-one glue and sealer—or you can use a glue stick), try covering your cardboard in wrapping paper or comic book pages before tracing shapes and cutting them out. This will add some cool designs to your cardboard stackers.

PAPER BAG PUPPET SHOW

WHAT YOU'LL NEED

- 1 paper lunch bag
- 2 to 3 sheets colorful construction paper
- Pencil
- Scissors
- Double-sided tape

Transform paper lunch bags into lively characters. Whether you are reenacting Shakespeare, your favorite TV show, or a play you wrote yourself, these fun puppets will help you put on an amazing performance. continued >>

23

INSTRUCTIONS

1. Begin by folding your paper bag so it lies flat. The bottom flap of the bag will be the puppet's mouth. Set the bag aside.

2. Next, cut out colorful pieces of paper to make eyes, a nose, teeth, and a mouth. You can sketch these shapes onto the paper before you cut them out or trace items like small jars to make things like round eyes. Be sure to notice the size of your bag so the puppet's features will fit on their "head." You don't want to end up with silly, tiny eyes! (Or do you?)

3. Now it is time to cut out some hair. To make fringe hair, fold a sheet of paper in half and compare it to the size of your bag; the hair will sit on your puppet like bangs in the front, and it will be long in the back.

4. Using your scissors, cut long, thin strips on both sides of the fold, leaving an uncut section at the fold that will go over the top of the bag. You may need to give your puppet a haircut to trim the bangs.

5. Using double-sided tape, attach the features you made to the bottom flap of your bag.

6. To use your puppet, stick your arm inside the opening of the bag and put your hand around the fold that forms the bottom to work the mouth.

CRAFTY RE-CREATION: With a large sheet of poster board or a large box, make a puppet theater. Fold the poster board in thirds so there is a front portion and two sides. Use scissors to cut out a space in the front part to put on your show.

CRAFT UP: If you've got yarn and glue, you've got fun puppet hair. Happen to have googly eyes lying around? Add them to your puppet. No construction paper? No problem! You can use paint or markers to make the puppet face.

CARDSTOCK CACTUS

WHAT YOU'LL NEED

- 4 sheets cardstock in shades of green
- Pencil
- Scissors
- Double-sided tape
- 1 cardboard toilet paper tube

You won't need a green thumb, water, or sunlight for this cactus. Instead, grab some scissors and green paper for this crafty "gardening" project.

INSTRUCTIONS

1. Begin by deciding what shape cactus you'd like to make. Some cacti are short, round, and stubby. Others are tall and thin.

2. Draw and cut out four of the same shape, all with flat bottoms.

3. Fold each of those pieces in half lengthwise (hot dog style).

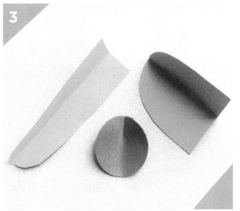

4. Use double-sided tape to attach two pieces to each other along the sides. Repeat with the other two pieces.

5. With more double-sided tape, attach the two pieces you just stuck together with the flat sides meeting. This gives you a 3D paper plant.

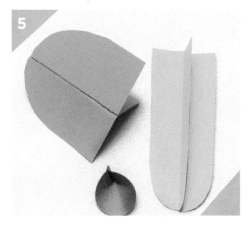

continued >>

6. Next, make a pot for your cactus. Set your 3D cactus on top of a cardboard toilet paper tube. Using a pencil, mark the 4 spots where the plant touches the tube.

7. With scissors, cut slits about ½ inch long into the tube. This will enable your cactus to sit inside its cardboard pot.

8. Line up the plant with the slits and insert it into the tube.

CRAFTY RE-CREATION: Try making a succulent, too. Cut out several circles of paper. Pinch one end of a circle together and use glue or double-sided tape to hold it in place. Repeat several times. Layer the circles into a cardboard toilet paper tube using glue to create the effect of a small succulent.

CRAFT UP: For more realistic plants, bust out the paint, crayons, or markers. Add contrasting shades of green and pops of yellow. Draw thorns on the cactus. Take a walk outside to find inspiration.

FOLDED FLICK FOOTBALL

WHAT YOU'LL NEED

• 1 sheet brown paper

Take it to the Super Bowl of crafts with an origami flick football. All you need is a sheet of paper and a strong finger flick to be the MVP of this project.

continued >>

INSTRUCTIONS

1. Fold the sheet of paper in half lengthwise (hot dog style).

2. Now your paper is a long rectangle. Fold both the top corners down to meet the folded edge, making a triangle.

3. Fold that triangle shape over to the right so that the bottom point meets the bottom edge of the rectangle of paper. This will make a second triangle of paper on top of the first.

4. Fold the triangle shape in a third time. This time, the outer edge of the triangle will meet the top edge of the rectangle. There should be a small rectangle of paper left below the triangle shape you folded.

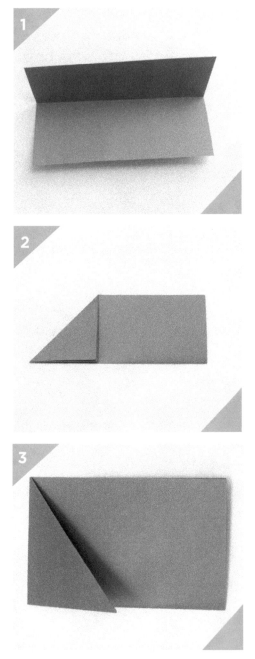

5. With that rectangle of paper, fold the two corners in toward the center to make another triangle shape.

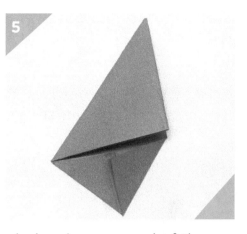

6. Tuck this smaller triangle into the bottom folds of the larger triangle.

7. Play with your flick football by balancing one end of the football on a flat surface and the other under your finger. The folded flat edge of the football should face your body. Toss the football across the table by flicking the triangle. Your opponent can make the shape of a goal post with their fingers. Take turns and see who can score the most goals.

CRAFTY RE-CREATION: For one-on-one practice with your football, make an entire mini football field. Straws or Popsicle sticks glued together make great goal posts. A green sheet of paper acts as the field.

CRAFT UP: To create a more realistic football, use a white paint marker or gel pen to draw stitching. Or use a lighter-weight paper to make a smaller football. Repeat the first step twice so that your beginning rectangle is thinner. This will also mean more triangular folds.

STRAW SPUTNIK

WHAT YOU'LL NEED

- 4 paper straws
- Scissors
- Ruler
- Pencil
- Circular objects for tracing, such as cups and jars
- 3 sheets colorful cardstock or scrapbooking paper
- Clear adhesive tape
- Glue stick

This craft was inspired by Sputnik, the first satellite that humans launched into space. Will yours become an asteroid, a space satellite, or a galactic paper sculpture? This out-of-this-world project can be all three. Display your satellite on a shelf with all your favorite space collectibles, or hang it from the ceiling.

INSTRUCTIONS

1. Cut the paper straws into shorter straws that are each about 3 inches long. Set aside.

2. Trace two 4-inch circles on a piece of colorful paper. Consider tracing an object like a large jar.

3. Trace two smaller circles on the colored paper, and then trace two more that are even smaller. Cups or small jars work great for this step.

4. Cut out all six paper circles.

5. Place one of the largest circles on a flat surface. If the paper is printed on only one side, have the unprinted side facing up.

6. Arrange eight straw pieces on the paper circle in the shape of a starburst, all touching at the center. Tape the straws to the paper.

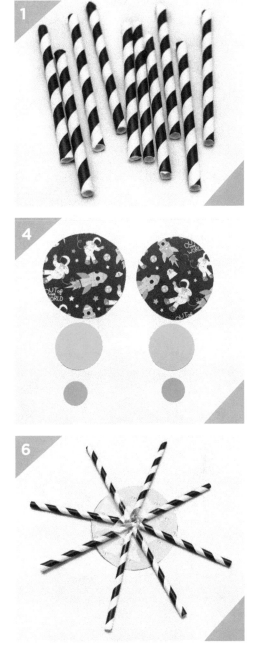

continued >>

7. Fold a piece of tape into a circle to give yourself something that is sticky on both sides. Place that tape in the center of the straws.

8. Attach the second large circle of paper to that tape, with the printed side (if there is one) facing up. This will create a paper sandwich with straws in the center.

9. Use the glue stick to attach the second largest circles of paper to the centers of both sides. Repeat with the smallest circles.

CRAFTY RE-CREATION: Small party plates are great for the large, primary circle of the Sputnik. If you don't have straws, roll tubes around a pencil using old magazine pages, as described in Picture-Perfect Frame (page 45). This has the added fun of bringing new colors and patterns to your spacey creation.

CRAFT UP: If you have aluminum foil in the pantry, you can take your sputnik into outer orbit. Using a glue stick, add a sheet of foil to the larger paper circles. Foil will also easily wrap around your straws.

PAPER PLATE WALL POCKET

WHAT YOU'LL NEED

- 2 paper plates the same size
- Scissors
- Pencil
- 1 sheet cardstock
- Double-sided tape
- Washi tape
- 8 inches yarn
- Clear adhesive tape

Next time you see a stack of paper plates in the cupboard, think beyond picnics and backyard barbecues. Instead think easy storage for your craft supplies and new room decor. The size of your wall pocket will depend on what size paper plates you use. Choose the largest and thickest plates you can get.

continued >>

35

INSTRUCTIONS

1. Cut one of the plates in half with scissors. You'll only need one whole plate and one half-plate to finish this project.

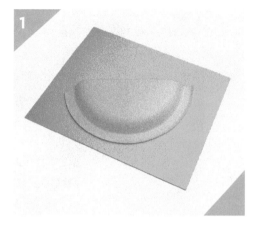

2. Use the other plate as a guide to trace a circle onto the cardstock. Cut out the circle.

3. Attach the circle to the inside center of the uncut plate with double-sided tape. (Depending on how much the plate curves, your circle may need to be smaller than the whole plate.)

4. Use washi tape to decorate the bottom (not the side food would go on) of the plate you cut in half. You can create any patterns or designs you'd like.

5. Place the uncut plate with the cardstock inside on a flat surface with the cardstock facing up. Put the half plate with the washi tape facing you on top on the first plate. The space between the two plates creates the pocket.

6. Join the two plates together by placing double-sided tape around the outside of the half circle where the edges meet.

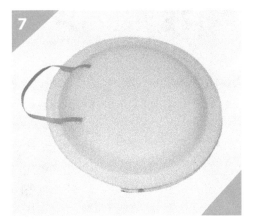

7. Add a small loop of yarn to the back and secure it with clear adhesive tape to create a hanger.

CRAFTY RE-CREATION: The strength of your paper plate wall pocket depends on the type of plate and the strength of the double-sided tape. Reinforce your wall pocket by using colorful duct tape around the outer edge. Follow steps 1 through 5 to assemble your wall pocket, then wrap the entire lower half in duct tape.

CRAFT UP: This project also works great with leftover party plates that already have designs on them. You will only see the design on the plate that is not cut in half, so consider decorating the half plate with paint or markers to match.

PRIZE RIBBON

WHAT YOU'LL NEED

- 3 to 5 sheets colorful paper
- Ruler
- Pencil
- Scissors
- Double-sided tape
- Circular objects for tracing, such as cups and jars

These prize ribbons make great gifts. For example, on Father's Day, let Dad know he's number one with a prize ribbon you made for him. Give these ribbons to teachers, family, and friends. Everyone loves to win an award! Even silly situations can be award-worthy. What can you think of?

INSTRUCTIONS

1. Measure four 4½-by-6-inch rectangles on sheets of colorful paper. Cut them out.

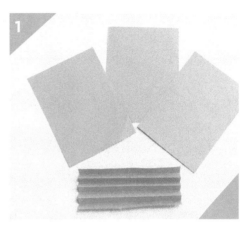

2. Begin with one rectangle, setting the others aside. Fold it in half lengthwise (hot dog style). Make a sharp crease along the fold.

3. Fold the rectangle in half lengthwise again and crease firmly. Fold in half lengthwise one more time, then unfold the rectangle.

4. Use the fold lines as a guide to accordion-fold the rectangle, folding one part up and one part down.

5. Repeat steps 2 through 4 with the remaining three rectangles.

6. When you have four accordion-folded sheets, fold them each in half widthwise (hamburger style). You will have four butterfly shapes.

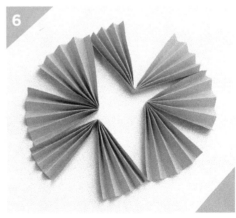

continued >>

7. Use a small piece of double-sided tape to attach the inside edges of the wings of each butterfly. This will give you four mini fan shapes.

8. Place a piece of double-sided tape along the outer edge of one half of the first fan shape and attach it to a second fan shape. Repeat until you have joined the four fan shapes to form a circle.

9. On the rest of your colorful paper, use bottles, small cups, or other round objects to trace three circles of different sizes. Cut them out.

10. Use double-sided tape to attach the largest circle to the fan circle. Stack the second smallest circle on top of the larger circle, and then the last.

11. Next, make the ribbon that hangs down. Draw two large rectangles on colorful paper and cut them out. Trim a triangle shape from the bottom of each rectangle to make it look like a ribbon.

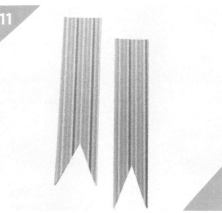

12. Use tape to attach the two ribbons to the back of the fan circle.

CRAFTY RE-CREATION: Personalize your prize ribbons by decorating the center of each ribbon to match the occasion. You can write what the award is for, add a photo, or cut out and tape (or draw) someone's initials in the center.

CRAFT UP: If you have fabric or ribbon, these make a great mixed media project. ("Mixed media" means combining mediums, such as paper and fabric.) Make the fan circle with paper, then experiment with fabric or ribbon for the ribbons that hang down.

NOTEBOOK WITH NOOKS

WHAT YOU'LL NEED

- Ruler
- 7 sheets colorful paper
- Pencil
- Scissors
- 1 paper lunch bag
- 2 rubber bands

Making your own pocket-size notebook—with nooks for storing ticket stubs, stickers, or photos—is about as easy as folding a sheet of paper. Change up the size, shape, and color of these useful notebooks to create things that are personal to you.

INSTRUCTIONS

1. With the ruler, measure and draw a 5-by-8-inch rectangle on each piece of paper. Cut out each rectangle and set it aside.

2. Next, prepare the paper bag, which will add nooks and storage pockets to your notebook. Use scissors to cut off about 4 inches from the top of the paper bag and about 1 inch from the bottom, so it is 5 inches long.

3. Fold all 7 sheets of paper and the bag in half horizontally (hamburger style).

4. Stack the paper and the bag in the order you want them to be in your notebook. Remember, the bag will become little pockets between the paper writing pages.

continued >>

5. When the pieces are in the order you want, use the rubber bands to hold everything together. Slip a rubber band over one of the long ends and slide it to the middle until you reach the center fold, which will be the spine of your notebook. Add a second rubber band to secure things tightly.

CRAFTY RE-CREATION: When you choose your paper, think about what you will use your notebook for. If you might later want to paint in your notebook, try using heavy paper like cardstock. If you want to make notes or create a field journal, consider sheets of lined notebook paper.

CRAFT UP: Book binding is a fun hobby with tons of creative possibilities. Play around to discover different methods for binding the pages together, like using a large craft needle and thread. Experiment with different cover options, like old cereal boxes.

PICTURE-PERFECT FRAME

WHAT YOU'LL NEED

- 2 sheets construction paper
- Ruler
- Pencil
- Scissors
- Double-sided tape
- Lightweight cardboard
- 8 paper straws
- Clear adhesive tape

Made from paper straws and an old cereal box, this custom picture frame can be the perfect match for your soccer team photo, favorite picture of Grandma, or an epic snap of you and your friends at the beach. continued >>

INSTRUCTIONS

1. Cut the construction paper across the short side into 2½-inch-wide strips. You'll need four strips.

2. Roll each strip around the pencil the long way, to create long cylindrical straw shapes. Hold the paper tight against the pencil as you roll.

3. When you reach the far end of the strip, secure the paper roll with double-sided tape on the inside edges. Repeat with all four strips and set aside.

4. Using a ruler, measure out a 6-by-8-inch rectangle on the piece of cardboard. In the center of that, measure out a smaller rectangle that is 4-by-6 inches.

5. Cut out both rectangles so that you are left with a frame of cardboard.

6. Lay three strips of double-sided tape side by side on one of the shorter sides of the frame.

7. To the tape, attach two paper straws and one of the paper tubes you made. You may wish to alternate between straws and paper tubes to create a pattern.

8. With scissors, trim the paper tubes and the straws so that the ends are even with the edges of the frame. Repeat on the opposite side.

9. To cover the two long sides, measure and trim the straws and paper rolls to about 6½ inches so that they will fit into the remaining open space.

10. Use clear adhesive tape to attach a photo to the back of the frame, taping it around all four sides.

CRAFTY RE-CREATION: No paper straws? No problem! You can replace the straws with more construction paper tubes. Or, if you have a bag of paper straws and no colorful paper, skip the tube-rolling and go straight to frame-making.

CRAFT UP: The instructions create a frame that fits a 4-by-6-inch photo. Adjust step 4 to make your frame fit any picture. Also, for a picture frame that sits on a desk, use a small, thick cardboard box, like a small gift box the size of your frame. Attach the frame to the side of the box using double sided tape. Set the box on your flat surface with the frame facing out to display.

CUSTOM CARDBOARD AIRPLANE

WHAT YOU'LL NEED

- Cardboard box
- Marker
- Ruler
- Scissors
- Washi tape

Have you ever dreamed of owning an airplane? This is your chance! The catch is that this plane is made of cardboard. The bonus is that you can have an entire fleet. Customize the shape, size, and color of your planes to make them all your own.

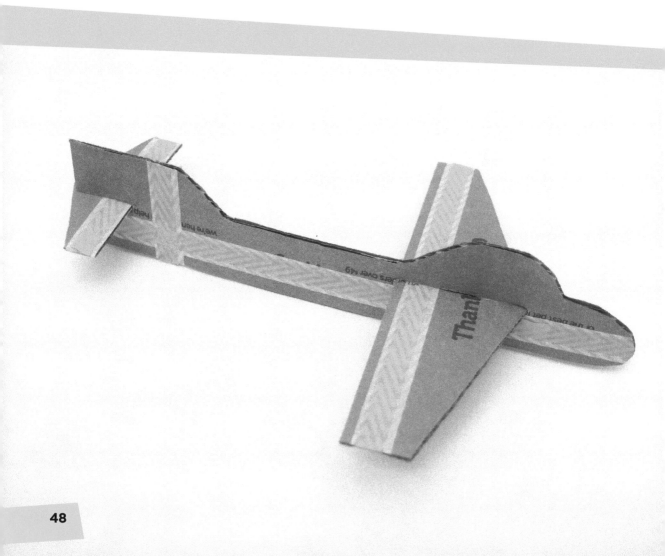

INSTRUCTIONS

1. Break down the cardboard box so you have one large, flat piece of cardboard. Ask for help from an adult if you need it.

2. On the cardboard, draw the outline of the body of an airplane, about 10 inches long. Draw a round bulge for a cockpit and a wide back end for the tail of the plane.

3. Next, draw a wing shape that is about 8 inches long. The wing should be a long, skinny pentagon: flat on three sides with a triangular point on top.

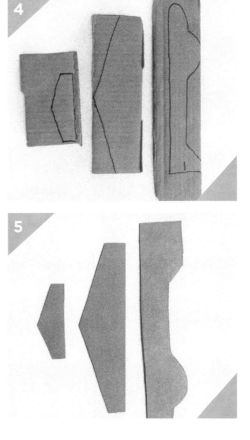

4. Draw a 4-inch-wide tail onto the cardboard. The tail of the plane should have the same pentagon shape as the wing but will be half as long.

5. Cut out the body, wing, and tail with scissors.

6. Measure the width of the widest section of the wing, where the triangular side comes to a point. Draw a line on the side of the plane that is the same length as the width you just measured. This line will be where the wing goes, so it should be centered near the front.

continued >>

7. Draw a 1-inch line at the end of the plane. This is where the tail will go.

8. Using scissors, cut slits along the two marks you just drew.

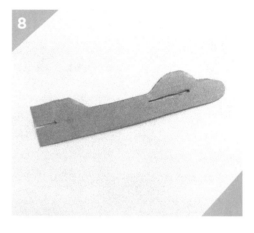

9. Decorate the plane, wings, and tail with washi tape on both sides.

10. To assemble the plane, insert the wing through the large slit in the middle of the plane, with the triangle pointing front toward the nose. Insert the smaller tail piece into the smaller slit, this time with the triangle pointing backward. Your plane is ready for departure!

CRAFTY RE-CREATION: You've heard of jumbo jets, right? The bigger your starting piece of cardboard, the bigger your plane can be. Bigger cardboard planes are heavier and may be less likely to fly, but they are still fun to play with.

CRAFT UP: It's a bird, it's a plane, it's a cardboard whatever you want! Using these same steps, you can build beyond planes. Make your flying piece of cardboard into a bird, dragon, or pterodactyl. Use paint, tape, or markers to decorate any creature you want.

PAPER CHAIN WALL ART

WHAT YOU'LL NEED

- 5 sheets cardstock in various colors
- Ruler
- Pencil
- Scissors
- Double-sided tape
- 1 cardboard paper towel tube
- 2 thumbtacks
- 3 feet yarn

If you have paper, scissors, and tape, you can make a paper chain. One chain is fun, but several in coordinating colors turn into an easy-to-make art installation.

continued >>

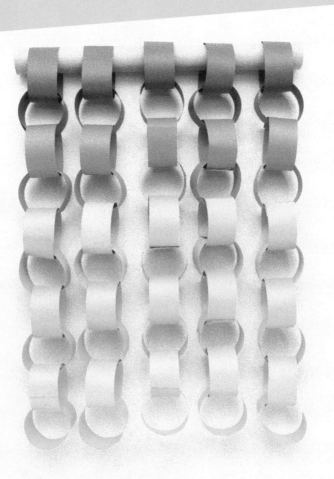

INSTRUCTIONS

1. Select five sheets of cardstock in either variations of the same color or colors that go together, such as all blues or greens and browns.

2. Using a ruler and pencil, measure and draw ten 1½-by-8-inch strips on each sheet of cardstock.

3. Cut out all 50 strips.

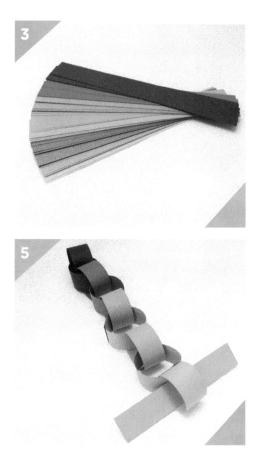

4. Starting with the darkest shade, bend one strip into a circle. Place a small piece of double-sided tape on one end to join it.

5. Lace another strip of the same color into the first circle before closing it with tape.

6. Continue with two strips of the next darkest shade, then two strips of the next darkest after that, and so on until you have a chain of 10 loops.

7. Make four more chains, so you have five chains of 10 loops each.

8. Use your cardboard paper towel tube as the hanger. Thread the first link of one chain onto the tube and use a piece of double-sided tape on the inside top part of the loop to attach it to the tube.

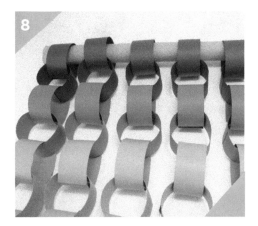

9. Repeat with the other four chains.

10. To finish your hanger, poke two thumbtacks into the tube and affix it to the wall. Be sure to ask permission before poking pins into any surface. Alternatively, thread a piece of yarn through the hole in the tube. The length should be about double the length of the tube. Bring the two ends of the yarn together and knot them. Slide the knot into the tube to hide it.

CRAFTY RE-CREATION: Skip the ombre effect and try making a chain with colorful strips of magazine, pages from your art journal, or even junk mail. Colorful paper is all around you!

CRAFT UP: Think of your paper chain as a graph. You can plot a design or symbol by drawing out your design first. Use a ruler to create a graph on a sheet of paper. Draw your design into the squares so you know where you need what color paper in the chain. Basic designs work best.

FOLDED FORTUNE TELLER

WHAT YOU'LL NEED

- 1 sheet printer paper
- Scissors
- Pen

Predict the future with a folded origami fortune teller. When you're ready, ask a friend to pick a color from the four showing. Move your fingers front and back and side to side to match the number of letters in that color. For example, R-E-D would be three movements. Let your friend look inside and choose a number. Move your fingers again the number of times they chose. Finally, your friend will choose another number. Lift the flap and reveal their fortune!

INSTRUCTIONS

1. Begin by trimming your paper into a perfect square. To do so, lay the sheet of paper flat, fold the top corner until it lines up perfectly with the opposite edge, and crease the fold, making a large triangle. Use scissors to cut off the excess rectangle of paper at the bottom.

2. Unfold the triangle and fold the other top corner to the other edge of the paper, once again creasing the fold. Open the paper back into a square; the creases should divide your paper into four equal triangles.

3. With your paper on a flat surface, fold all four corners in to the center (one at a time, creasing the folds as you go). There should be a spot where the first two creases you made meet, like the center point of an X. This is where you want the tips of all the triangles to be.

4. Flip the new, smaller square over so the folds you made are facing down.

continued >>

5. Repeat step 3, folding all the corners in to the center to make four little triangles.

6. Now you have a smaller square. Fold it in half crosswise (hamburger style), crease it, and unfold it. Then fold it in half lengthwise (hot dog style), crease it, and unfold it again. This step makes the fortune teller more flexible and easier to use.

7. Pick up the paper. The first set of folds created small pockets where your fingers will go. With some gentle manipulation, the points of the second set of folds should meet in the center.

8. Now, lay your shape lay flat again. It is time to write in the fortunes! On the first triangles you made, write out the names of four different colors.

9. On each side of the fold of second triangles you made, write a number under 20.

10. Lift the flaps of the second set of triangles and write short fortunes underneath, such as *You will be a* New York Times *bestselling author, You will be drafted into the NFL,* or *You will star in a movie with a talking dog*.

11. When each triangle includes a fortune, it's time to start predicting the future! Slide your fingers into the pockets so that the colors you wrote are visible and the "mouth" of the fortune teller is closed. Then follow the directions at the top of this craft.

CRAFTY RE-CREATION: Next time you get fortune cookies, save the fortunes. You can tape the little slips of paper into your fortune teller or use those fortunes to inspire your own.

CRAFT UP: If you're more into puppets than you are telling fortunes, this is still a craft for you! Add eyes to two of the corners, paint a tongue inside, and you have a perfect puppet (or a snake head, as on page 70).

PLANETARY PAPER

WHAT YOU'LL NEED

- 9 sheets cardstock in various colors
- Circular objects for tracing, such as cups and jars
- Pencil
- Scissors
- Double-sided tape
- Large craft needle
- 10 to 12 feet yarn

Set out on an exploration of the solar system. In this project, paper balls of different sizes and colors correspond with the eight planets and the sun. If you want to include everyone's favorite dwarf planet, Pluto, add another sheet of cardstock.

INSTRUCTIONS

1. Find a picture of the solar system online or in a book. Use this to guide what color of paper you'd like to use for each planet. For example, you might choose red for Mars.

2. When you have selected a color for each planet and the sun, trace four circles of the same size onto each piece of cardstock. Use different sizes of cups and bowls to trace the different planets, and look at your picture to decide how large to make each planet. The largest circle should be the sun.

3. Cut out all the circles you traced. You should have 36 in total (40 if you decide to add Pluto!).

4. Fold each circle in half so the sides you want to show face inward.

continued >>

5. To assemble the planets, begin with four folded circles of the same color. Set two aside. With the other two, use double-sided tape to attach one of the circle halves to a half of the second circle. Attach the sides you don't want to show, and make sure to line them up. Repeat with the other two circles of the same color.

6. You now have two halves of a planet that look like a circle with a half circle sticking up. Using double-sided tape, attach the two flat surfaces together, taking care to not put tape in the very center. You now have a 3D planet.

7. Repeat steps 5 and 6 for all the planets and the sun.

8. Time to connect the solar system! Thread a large craft needle with a piece of yarn. Start with the planet you'd like to come last in the solar system. Pull the yarn through the center of the ball. Tie a knot in the yarn under the planet so the yarn won't slip through.

9. Move up the piece of yarn a little way and tie another knot there so your next planet will not slide down.

10. String the next planet onto the yarn. It should rest on the second knot you made. Continue until all planets and the sun are strung. Leave enough yarn at the top for hanging your solar system.

CRAFTY RE-CREATION: If you are short on paper, you could always make your planets flat circles. Just trace one circle for each planet, cut, and color. These would be better pinned to a bulletin board or taped to a wall rather than hung.

CRAFT UP: Create a planetary mobile by hanging each of your planets from a separate piece of yarn. When you are finished, tie all the strings to a wire coat hanger and hang your mobile from a hook or from the ceiling.

CONFETTI-FILLED BOOKMARK

WHAT YOU'LL NEED

- Ruler
- Clear packing tape
- 2 to 5 sheets cardstock in different colors
- Pencil
- Scissors
- Hole punch
- Clear adhesive tape

Grab a few office supplies from around the house to create a confetti-filled bookmark that will give you a great excuse to crack open your favorite book.

INSTRUCTIONS

1. Use a ruler to measure the width of your packing tape. The width varies among brands but is usually around 2 inches.

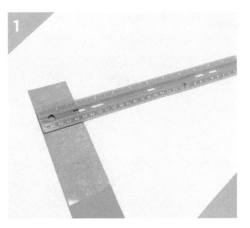

2. Cut a strip of colorful cardstock that is 8 inches long and the same width as the packing tape. Set the cardstock strip aside.

3. Cut a strip of packing tape that is 8 inches long. Gently place the tape on a flat surface, like a table, with the sticky side up.

4. Cut a second 8-inch strip of packing tape and carefully lay it on top of the other strip, so the two sticky sides stick to each other. This is the laminated front for your bookmark. Set it aside.

5. Use a hole punch to create confetti circles from colorful cardstock paper. Set them aside.

continued >>

6. Cut an 8-inch strip of clear adhesive tape and carefully lay it on a flat surface, sticky side up. Place your cardstock strip on the tape so it covers just half the width of the tape. Place the laminated strip you made from packing tape on top of the cardstock and fold the clear adhesive tape over it. Repeat this step on the other long side and one of the short sides of the cardstock strip. Now you have a pouch with the cardstock strip on one side and the laminated packing tape strip on the other side, and one short side still open.

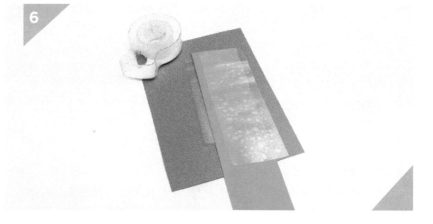

7. Fill the pouch with the confetti you created.

8. Use one last piece of clear adhesive tape to seal off the open side of the bookmark.

CRAFTY RE-CREATION: Packing tape is an underrated craft supply. Not only can it be used to create a clear pouch where confetti can fly freely, but the sticky side also has creative possibilities. Try making bookmarks by placing items such as dried leaves or feathers on a strip of cardstock and applying a piece of packing tape to secure everything in place. DIY laminating!

CRAFT UP: Hole punches come in more shapes than just circles. If you're lucky, you might have some that punch stars or squares. No hole punch to be found? Don't worry! Use scissors to cut confetti by making tiny strips or triangles of paper.

PAPER WEAVING

WHAT YOU'LL NEED

- 1 sheet cardstock
- Ruler
- Pencil
- Scissors
- Colorful paper
- Magazines
- Clear adhesive tape

You probably know that people weave baskets, blankets, and clothes. Did you know you can also weave paper? This is a great project for using up scraps of colorful paper and recycling old magazines.

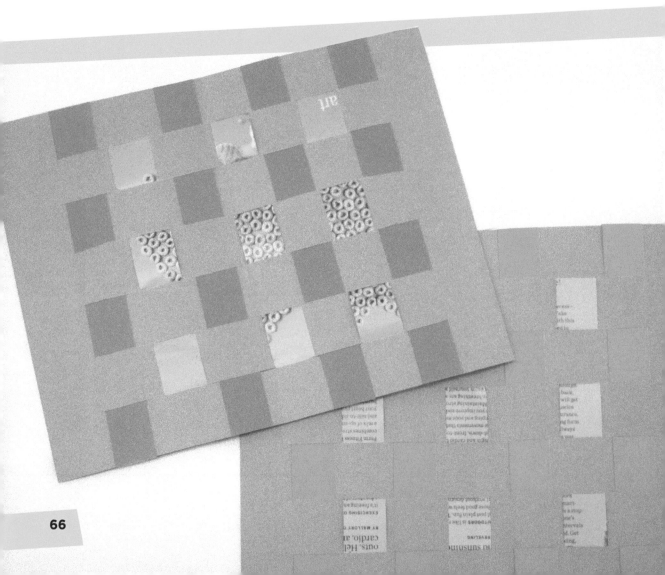

INSTRUCTIONS

1. Place the cardstock on a flat surface. Using a ruler and a pencil, draw a 1-inch-wide border around the whole sheet of cardstock. This will create a frame for the edge of your weaving.

2. Fold the cardstock in half hamburger style, with your border on the outside. Use the ruler to draw four lines, each 1 inch apart, within the border. Leave the outside border blank.

3. With the cardstock still folded in half, cut through both halves along the lines you just drew. Start the cuts in the center of the page (on the folded edge) and cut to the top border. Don't cut past the border line. Set the cardstock aside.

continued >>

4. Use a ruler and scissors to cut out 1-inch-wide strips along the long side of the colorful paper and from pages of the magazines. You will need about five strips of each, for a total of 10.

5. Unfold the cardstock and place it on a flat surface.

6. Grab one of the strips of colorful paper and begin weaving it into the cardstock. Go over the border, then under the next strip. Repeat the pattern of over and under until you get to the other edge of the cardstock.

7. Continue to weave. Alternate between strips of colored paper and strips from the magazine. If the first strip started by going over the border, the next should start by going under. Repeat this pattern with all the strips of paper.

8. When you have reached the bottom of the cardstock frame, you may need to slightly adjust the pieces you wove to make them evenly spaced.

9. Use tape to attach the woven strips to the back of the cardstock frame. Then use scissors to trim off any strips that stick out beyond the frame.

CRAFTY RE-CREATION: To weave a more intricate design, cut the slits into the cardstock closer together and make your paper strips thinner. For more variation in pattern and colors, use magazine pages for all the strips, or try paper in your favorite team's colors.

CRAFT UP: The Confetti-Filled Bookmark on page 62 uses packing tape to laminate. Use that technique to turn your paper weaving into a place mat or coasters (they make great gifts!). Cover both sides of the weaving with clear packing tape. Overlap the tape strips for a good seal. After "laminating," you can either leave it as it is to use as a place mat or cut the weaving into squares or circles to create coasters.

PAPER CHAIN PYTHON

WHAT YOU'LL NEED

- 5 sheets cardstock, in two shades of green
- Ruler
- Pencil
- Scissors
- Coin, for tracing
- Double-sided tape
- 1 sheet construction paper
- Clear packing tape

If you've ever dreamed of having a pet snake, here's your chance to make your very own. Who knew paper chains could be so verssssssatile!

INSTRUCTIONS

1. Select two different shades of green cardstock for the body of the snake. You will need 2 sheets of each color for the body, as well as another sheet for the head.

2. Using a ruler, measure and draw four rectangles on each piece of cardstock for the body. The rectangles should be about 1½ inches wide and 8 inches long. Cut out all eight rectangles.

3. Using a coin, trace circles in four rectangles that are the same color. Cut out the circles.

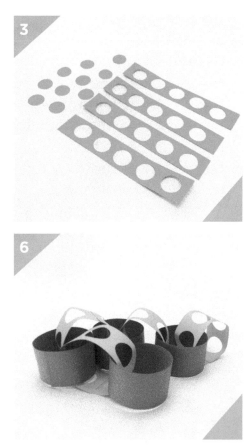

4. Take one of the rectangles that has a hole in it and bend it into a circle. Use a small piece of double-sided tape to fasten the circle so it stays closed.

5. Next, take a rectangle of the other shade of green and put it through the center of the first circle, so they form two interlocking circles. Close it with double-sided tape.

6. Alternating shades of green, continue building a chain until all eight rectangles are connected. Set aside.

continued >>

7. Follow the instructions for the Folded Fortune Teller (page 54) to make a snake head out of your last piece of cardstock.

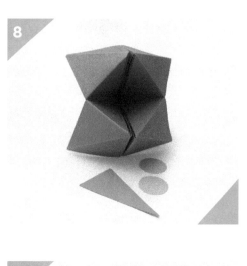

8. Using construction paper and double-sided tape, make a face for your snake. Don't forget the tongue!

9. Using packing tape, attach the snake head to the body. First, cut another coin-size hole in the first link of the chain to stick the snake head into. When the point of the head is through the hole, attach it with plenty of packing tape to hold it in place.

CRAFTY RE-CREATION: Is your favorite snake yellow and black? You can make a white paper snake into any color you want. Decorate before you cut your paper into strips.

CRAFT UP: Are you more of entomologist than a herpetologist? No problem! Make a caterpillar instead. Get creative by making dragons, eels, and worms. This process will work for any long and skinny creature you can imagine.

FOOTBALL MINI PIÑATA

WHAT YOU'LL NEED

- 1 roll brown crepe paper streamer
- Ruler
- Scissors
- 1 paper plate
- Double-sided tape
- Piñata fillings, such as candy or small toys

Piñatas are so much fun! Now you can make individual piñatas for your party guests. You don't beat these mini piñatas with a stick, but they are still full of fun. The instructions here are for a football-inspired piñata. Try this one first, then use your imagination to come up with other decoration ideas.

continued >>

INSTRUCTIONS

1. Cut a length of paper streamer about 1 foot long.

2. Fold the streamer in half lengthwise (hot dog style).

3. Use scissors to cut slits equal distance apart down the open edge (not the folded edge) of the folded streamer. Be careful not to cut all the way to the fold. This will give the streamer a fringe.

4. Unfold the streamer and cut down the center where the fold was, so you have two lengths of fringed streamer.

5. Repeat steps 1 though 4 a few times until you have a small pile of fringed streamers to work with. Set them aside.

6. Fold the paper plate in half. Close the edges together with double-sided tape, leaving a small opening on one end, near the fold. Make sure the opening is big enough for you to stuff things inside your piñata.

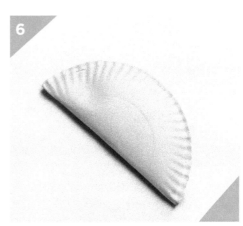

7. Starting at the folded end of the paper plate that does not have the opening, place a strip of double-sided tape across the paper plate from edge to edge. Attach some streamer to the tape. Tape the edge that is not fringed, so that the fridge side is free and pointing up.

8. Continue taping and adding fringe, moving across the folded paper plate and making sure the fringe is all pointing the same direction.

continued >>

9. When you're done, push some small toys, stickers, or candy through the opening you left. Use a piece of double-sided tape to close the hole.

CRAFTY RE-CREATION: If you're not a football fan, you can decorate the piñata like other things that are this same shape. Yellow streamers work great for tacos; add construction paper toppings along the rounded edge. Red streamers with green construction paper along the rounded edge can turn a paper plate into a watermelon slice.

CRAFT UP: Using white yarn and white glue, create the stitching on your football piñata for a more realistic look. Add one long piece of yarn and several smaller pieces perpendicular to it.

FLIP-BOOK FUN

- 10 sheets (or more!) colorful paper
- Ruler
- Pencil
- Scissors
- Double-sided tape
- 1 rubber band
- Glue stick

One book, a million different faces. Well, maybe not a million . . . that would be a really big book! But the more pages you add to your flip-book, the more options you'll have. What kind of faces will you create? Will they be handsome, scary, silly, or all of the above? continued >>

77

INSTRUCTIONS

1. Choose three sheets of paper of the same color. Trim them into 5-by-6-inch rectangles. Fold each trimmed sheet in half to make three 3-by-5-inch rectangles.

2. On a different color of paper, trace out six head shapes (just an oval is enough). Your flip-book will look the smoothest if all the heads are the same shape and color. Make sure the head shapes fit on the folded rectangles from step 1.

3. Cut out the head shapes.

4. Mark where the heads will go on each of the sheets of folded paper. The heads need to be in the exact same spot on each page.

5. Attach the heads to each page with double-sided tape.

6. Stack the folded sheets. Wrap a rubber band around the sheets so that it rests in the fold, creating a spine. This is the same technique you used on page 42 to make Notebooks with Nooks.

7. Using the ruler, draw lines to divide the first page into three sections (top, middle, and bottom), from the bound spine of the book out to the edge.

8. With scissors, cut the page across the lines you drew. Cut almost to the spine of the book, but not all the way! Use the first page you measured as a guide to cut the next page. Repeat with every page.

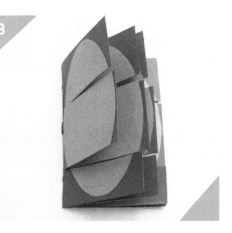

9. When the pages have all been cut, decorate each of the faces using facial features you cut out from pieces of colorful paper. Each of the three sections should show one part of a face: the top is hair, the middle is eyes and nose, and the bottom shows a mouth. They should all be different.

continued >>

10. Glue the features onto your faces.

11. Flip the pages to mix and match faces.

CRAFTY RE-CREATION: If you have a stack of magazines, this can be a fun collage project. Cut out eyes, hair, noses, and mouths from magazines to make your own crazy faces. Tape or glue the features into your flip-book. Just remember to keep the three sections of the face the same as described.

CRAFT UP: Add detail to the faces you create using paint, markers, or crayons. Illustrate your faces before you bind your book and cut the sections. As you illustrate, remember the three sections of the face for when you flip pages.

BAG OF STARS

WHAT YOU'LL NEED

- 9 paper lunch bags
- Scissors
- Pencil
- Double-sided tape
- Paper clip

Brown paper bags aren't just for taking your lunch to school. Turn boring brown bags into stars for personalized room improvement or amazing party decorations. continued >>

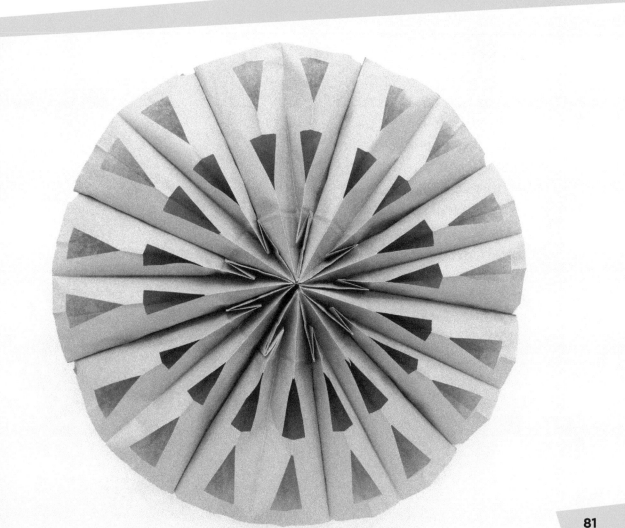

INSTRUCTIONS

1. Fold the lunch bags flat and stack them on top of one another other so the bottoms are all facing the same way.

2. Take one bag from the top of the pile. Using scissors, cut out two small half triangles in one side of the bag. Make sure not to cut too far into the bag; you don't want to cut all the way to the center fold.

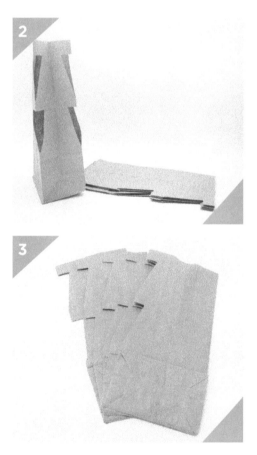

3. Lay the cut bag on top of the next bag in the stack and trace where the triangles are. Cut out the traced triangles on the bag. Repeat on all the bags.

4. Stack the bags again. Make sure all the cut parts line up and trim as necessary.

5. Take one bag from the stack and lay it on a flat surface.

6. Begin taping the bags together. First, make an upside-town T shape on the bag out of double-sided tape. The top of the T should run along the bottom edge of the bag and the center stripe of the T should run along the center of the bag.

7. Stack the next bag directly on top, making sure the cut-out part is facing the same direction. Make another tape T on this bag, then stack the next one. Repeat on all the bags.

8. When you have taped the last bag, open the star to reveal your design. Do not tape the first and last bags together. Instead, use a paper clip to connect their edges. This way you can remove the clip to fold your star for storage.

continued >>

CRAFTY RE-CREATION: Paper lunch bags are a wonderfully unexpected craft supply. Use them to make a Paper Bag City like the one on page 4. Or create hand puppets as in Paper Bag Puppet Show (page 23). You can also add them to your Notebook with Nooks (page 42) to create handy pockets.

CRAFT UP: If you want to paint your bags before you get started, go for it! Let the paint dry before you start cutting and taping. Another fun trick is to use gift bags to create more colorful stars.

PAPER LANTERN

WHAT YOU'LL NEED

- 16 Popsicle sticks
- Double-sided tape
- 4 printed paper napkins
- Pencil
- Scissors
- LED tea light

Printed paper napkins are way too fun to use just to wipe the ketchup off your face. They are a great craft supply. Napkins are thin enough for light to shine through, making them perfect for crafting these tabletop paper lanterns.

continued >>

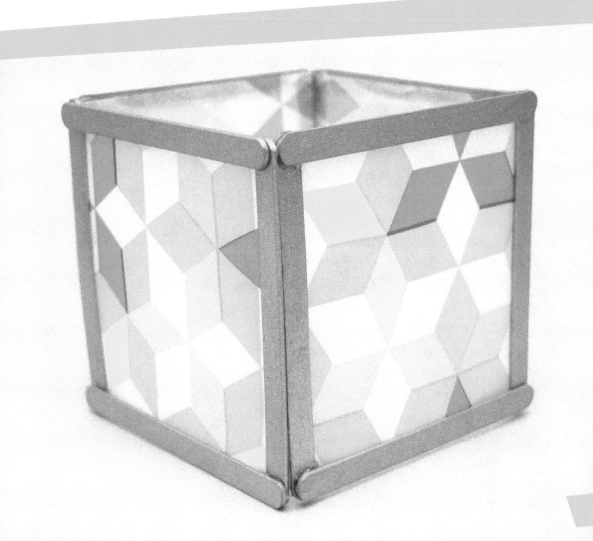

INSTRUCTIONS

1. Begin by placing two Popsicle sticks horizontally and parallel to each other on a flat surface; these will be the top and bottom edges of a square frame.

2. Put a small piece of double-sided tape on each end of these two Popsicle sticks.

3. Grab two more Popsicle sticks. Attach them to the first two sticks to make the sides of the square frame.

4. Repeat steps 1 through 3 with the rest of the Popsicle sticks so you have four square frames. These will form the four sides of the lantern.

5. Unfold a paper napkin and lay it printed side down on a flat surface. Place one square frame onto the napkin and trace the frame shape. Be sure to trace both the outside square and the inside square of the frame. Repeat with each napkin.

6. Cut out the napkin squares, cutting in between the two lines you traced. The square pieces of napkin you cut should come out slightly smaller than the outside of the frame, but big enough to not fall through the center of the frame.

7. Line the four frames up on a flat surface in a straight line. Apply strips of double-sided tape to all four Popsicle sticks of each square. Attach a square of napkin to each square frame, printed side down.

8. Run a piece of double-sided tape along the inner edge of one side of a frame. Position the tape so that only half of it is attached to the frame. The other half of the strip should hang off the edge.

9. Take a second square frame and line it up to create a right angle with the frame you just taped. Attach them together using the tape that you left hanging off the first frame.

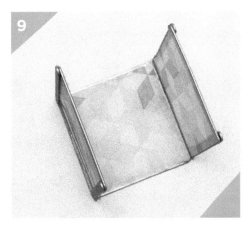

continued >>

10. Repeat with the remaining square frames until your cube-shaped lantern is built. Place a small LED light inside.

CRAFTY RE-CREATION: If you don't have Popsicle sticks, try a cardboard box. From the cardboard box, cut out four squares of the exact same size. Inside each of those squares cut out a slightly smaller square to create a cardboard frame. Then follow steps 5 through 12.

CRAFT UP: Experiment with wax paper for the colorful side panels of your lantern. Try pressing dried leaves between two sheets of wax paper and ironing the wax paper, or ironing crayon shavings between two sheets on a very low temperature to get a cool tie-dye effect. Ask an adult for help with the iron if needed.

FLYING PAPER PTERODACTYL

WHAT YOU'LL NEED

- 1 sheet glitter craft paper
- Ruler
- Pencil
- Scissors
- 2 to 3 sheets cardstock, in several colors
- Hole punch
- Clear adhesive tape
- Double-sided tape
- 1 small paper straw
- 1 paper straw large enough that the smaller one can fit inside

Have you ever seen a pterodactyl fly? You will soon. Prehistoric beasts take flight with your creativity (and some paper straws). Get ready for flying dinosaurs! continued >>

INSTRUCTIONS

1. Using glitter craft paper, draw and cut out the basic outline of a pterodactyl. Cut an oval for the body, two wing shapes, and a head. You don't want the creature to measure much taller than 2 inches.

2. From cardstock paper, cut out details to decorate the pterodactyl. Use a hole punch to create a circle for the eye, cut a jagged shape for teeth, and create small feet.

3. Tape everything together using a mix of clear and double-sided tape.

4. Cut the smaller of the two paper straws to about double the height of your pterodactyl, roughly 5 inches. Trim the larger straw so that it is about 1½ inches longer than the smaller straw. Set the long straw aside.

5. Pinch one end of the small straw so that the edges come together and tape it closed tightly with clear adhesive tape.

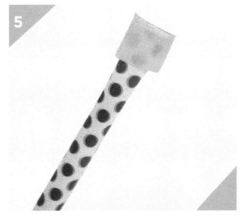

6. Tape this straw to the back of your pterodactyl with the closed end pointing up. Place the straw so that half of it is attached to the back of the pterodactyl and the other half is below your creature.

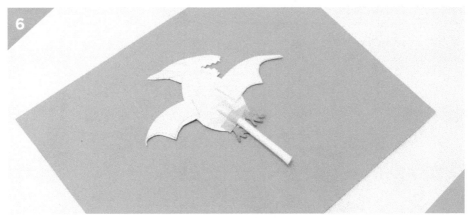

continued >>

Flying Paper Pterodactyl **91**

7. When you are ready for your pterodactyl to take flight, place the straw attached to the pterodactyl inside the larger straw. Tilt your head back and blow hard on the larger straw. This should send the creature flying!

CRAFTY RE-CREATION: If bats and birds are more your thing, those make great straw-propulsion flyers too. Rockets and planes are other options. Just switch up the design you cut out in step 1 and then follow the rest of the steps as written.

CRAFT UP: While glittery paper is fun, a plain sheet of white paper and some pens will work just as well to create the dinosaur of your dreams.

SWISS CHEESE STRING LIGHTS

WHAT YOU'LL NEED

- LED string lights
- 3 to 4 cardboard paper towel tubes, or 6 to 8 toilet paper tubes
- Scissors
- Hole punch
- Paintbrush
- Decoupage medium or white school glue
- 1 sheet colored tissue paper
- Clear adhesive tape

Level up your craft game using cardboard tubes to make a batch of mini lanterns. Colored tissue paper will set the mood. Looking for fun, spooky Halloween decorations? Try orange and black. Throwing a *Minecraft*-themed party? Try shades of green and brown tissue paper. Just make sure to use *only* LED lights—other lights could be a fire hazard. continued >>

INSTRUCTIONS

1. Begin by counting the lights on your set of LED string lights. You'll need one cardboard toilet paper tube for every two lights, or one paper towel roll for every four lights.

2. If you're using cardboard toilet paper tubes, cut them in half around the middle to make two mini tubes. If you're using paper towel rolls, cut them into quarters around the middle to make four mini tubes.

3. Now cut each mini tube along one side so it opens up. Unroll and flatten it with your hand.

4. Use a hole punch to make small holes in the flattened tubes, and trace larger circles and cut them out with scissors (or, if you have one, use a 1-inch circle punch). This will give your tubes a Swiss cheese effect. The more holes you cut, the more light will shine through.

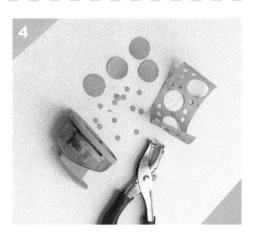

5. Using a paintbrush, apply decoupage medium or school glue to one side of the tubes. If one side of the cardboard has printing on it, apply the decoupage medium to that side.

6. With the decoupage medium side down, place the cardboard onto a sheet of tissue paper. Repeat for all the pieces. Allow to dry.

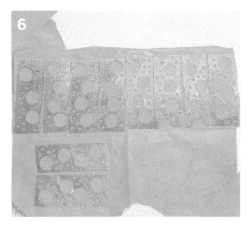

7. Trim the excess tissue paper from around the cardboard pieces.

continued >>

8. Bend the cardboard pieces back into tubes with the tissue paper side facing in and seal them using clear adhesive tape.

9. Add your tubes to the string lights by inserting a light bulb into one of the holes you punched. Push the light bulb through the tissue paper covering the hole. Most standard size LED string lights will fit perfectly and stay put. Add a bit of glue or tape around the hole, if needed. Plug in your lights and admire your work!

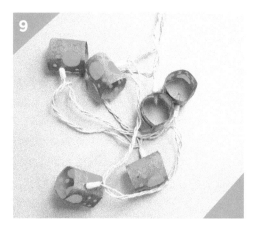

CRAFTY RE-CREATION: Hole punches come in many shapes and sizes. If you have different kinds, try mixing up the size and shape of your holes.

CRAFT UP: If you don't have colorful tissue paper, try colorful paper napkins. Any thin paper with a color or pattern will work great for this project.

ABOUT THE AUTHOR

JENNIFER PERKINS is a creative content designer living in Austin, Texas, with her husband, two children, and seven pets. Jennifer has had a lifelong passion for creating. She began her career as a jewelry designer and has taken many different artsy paths along the way, including those of television host, podcaster, and most recently kids' craft author. Her favorite crafty pastimes include art journaling, book binding, and anything involving pom-poms. When she does not have a paintbrush in her hand, she enjoys extreme holiday decorating and thrift store shopping.

9 798886 080551